The Young Violinist's Early Music Collection

Collection de musique ancienne du Jeune Violoniste
Alte Musik für junge Geiger

Ten gems for violin and piano · Dix joyaux pour violon et piano
Zehn Kostbarkeiten für Violine und Klavier

arranged by Edward Huws Jones

© 1996 by Faber Music Ltd
First published in 1996 by Faber Music Ltd
3 Queen Square London WC1N 3AU
Cover design by S & M Tucker
Music processed by Wessex Music Services
Printed in England by Halstan and Co Ltd
All rights reserved

ISBN 0 571 51669 6

Preface

Medieval and renaissance music has a tremendous vitality and immediacy – the sheer rhythmic energy suggests the world of jazz, and the purity of the melodic lines points to folk music. The sounds of early music are a far cry from the stuffiness and formality which young people sometimes associate with traditional concert repertoire!

The instrument we now know as the violin came into being during the early part of the 16th century. Much of the music in this collection was written long before then, and was intended for earlier types of bowed string instruments – for medieval fiddle, rebec and viol. But the music is so irresistibly string-like that we have every excuse to enjoy these pieces on the modern violin.

Our collection spans six centuries and a diversity of styles and this is reflected in the different types of accompaniment. Some, like the two Dowland dances, simply follow the original lute accompaniment; others, such as Monteverdi *Sinfonia*, have been given a keyboard part based on the original string ensemble. The earlier pieces, such as *Pour mon coeur* and *Trotto*, were originally played to drones or percussion and have had piano accompaniments added specially for this edition.

The accompaniments can of course be played on piano but also work well on other keyboard instruments. Particularly effective is an electronic keyboard using a harpsichord or chamber organ voice (such as recorder or pan-pipes).

Edward Huws Jones

Préface

La musique médiévale et la musique de la Renaissance ont un attrait et une vitalité immédiats; leur énergie rythmique évoque l'univers du jazz et la pureté de la ligne mélodique fait songer à la musique populaire. Les sonorités de la musique ancienne n'ont pas grand chose de commun avec la raideur et la sévérité que les jeunes associent parfois au répertoire de concert traditionnel.

L'instrument que nous désignons aujourd'hui sous le nom de violon vit le jour durant la première moitié du seizième siècle. Bon nombre des pièces du présent recueil furent écrites bien avant et destinées à des types antérieurs d'instruments à cordes et à archet, le violon, le rebec et la viole du Moyen Age. Mais cette musique se prête si bien aux cordes que nous sommes parfaitement excusables de l'appliquer au violon moderne.

La présente collection couvre six siècles et une grande variété de styles, ce que reflètent les différents types d'accompagnement. Certains morceaux, dont les deux danses de Dowland, se contentent de suivre l'accompagnement original de luth; mais d'autres, dont la *Sinfonia* de Monteverdi, ont été assortis d'une partie de clavier basée sur l'ensemble de cordes original. Les pièces antérieures, telles que *Pour mon coeur* et *Trotto*, furent initialement jouées avec des bourdons ou une percussion, et leur accompagnement de piano a été conçu pour la présente édition.

Les accompagnements peuvent bien-sûr être joués au piano mais ils conviennent aussi à d'autres types d'instruments à clavier. Nous recommandons notamment un clavier électronique pourvu d'un jeu de clavecin ou de positif (flûte à bec ou flûte de Pan).

Edward Huws Jones

Einleitung

Die Musik von Mittelalter und Renaissance hat unglaubliche Vitalität und Direktheit – die von ihr ausgehende rhythmische Energie ähnelt Elementen des Jazz, die Klarheit der melodischen Linien verweist auf Volksmusik. Der Klang dieser Musik ist unendlich weit entfernt von der Langeweile und Steifheit, die junge Menschen öfters mit dem herkömmlichen Konzertrepertoire assoziieren.

Die heutige Violine stammt aus dem frühen 16. Jahrhundert. Fast alle Werke der vorliegenden Sammlung entstanden vor dieser Zeit und waren für unterschiedliche ältere Streichinstrumente gedacht, für die mittelalterliche Fiedel, die Rebec und die Gambe. Die Musik ist aber so eindeutig für ein mit dem Bogen gestrichenes Instrument konzipiert, daß wir sie ohne weiteres auf der heutigen Geige spielen können.

Unsere Sammlung enthält Werke aus sechs Jahrhunderten und eine Vielzahl von Stilrichtungen, was sich in den unterschiedlichen Begleitsätzen niederschlägt. Die Begleitung entspricht teilweise, wie in den beiden Dowland-Tänzen, der ursprünglichen Lauten-Begleitung. Bei anderen Stücken, wie in der *Sinfonia* von Monteverdi, wurde die ursprüngliche Begleitung durch ein Streichersemble in einem Klavierauszug zusammengefaßt. Zu den frühen Stücken, wie etwa *Pour mon coeur* und *Trotto*, wurde ursprünglich eine Begleitung gesummt oder auf Schlaginstrumenten gespielt; für diese Werke wurden Klaviersätze eigens erstellt.

Die Begleitung kann selbstverständlich auf dem Klavier gespielt werden, aber auch andere Tasteninstrumente können zur Begleitung herangezogen werden. Besonders effektvoll ist die Begleitung auf einem Keyboard mit der Einstellung für Cembalo oder kleine Orgel (Blockflöten- oder Panpfeifen-Register).

Edward Huws Jones

Illustration acknowledgements

P4: By permission of the British Library MS Arundel 91 f21 8V.
P5 & cover: By permission of the Bibliothèque Royale Albert 1er Brussels
P6 & 13: By permission of the Master and Fellows of St. John's College, Cambridge.
P11: By permission of the British Library MS Royal Roll 14 BV

Pour mon Coeur

Anonymous
12th century French

The Frog Galliard

John Dowland
(1563 - 1626)

Noel Nouvelet

Anonymous
15th century French

Rhythmic, but not fast ♩ = 72

Sinfonia: I Tune the Lyre

Claudio Monteverdi
(1567 - 1643)

Scottish Brawl

Pierre Attaingnant
(d. c. 1550)

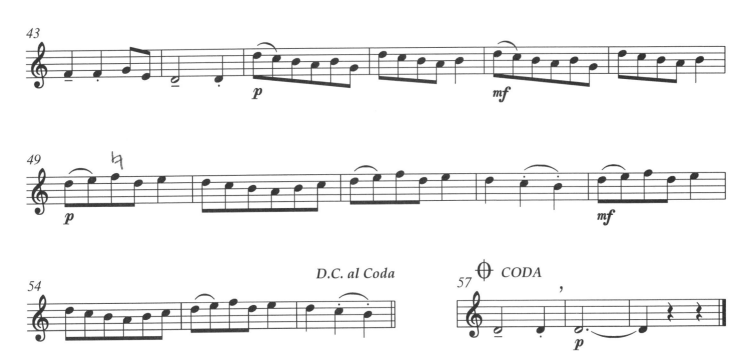

Passamezzo

Diego Ortiz
(b. c. 1510)

Lively ♩ = 92

14th March

Madrigal
[O felici occhi miei]

Diego Ortiz

Free and expressive ♩ = 69

Lachrimae Pavan

John Dowland

2nd May

Trotto

Anonymous
14th century Italian

Fast ♩. = 116

Galliard: The Fairie-round

Anthony Holborne
(d. 1602)

Springy, but not too fast ♩ = 104

mf

legato

7

p legato

12

f

19

senza rit.

p 2+3 *cresc.* 4 5+6+

f